TEAM

TEAM

Six Essentials for Building a Productive Team

BRENT ELDRIDGE

RESOURCE *Publications* · Eugene, Oregon

TEAM
Six Essentials for Building a Productive Team

Resource Publications
A Division of Wipf and Stock Publishers
199 W. 8th Ave., Suite 3
Eugene, OR 97401

www.wipfandstock.com

ISBN 13: 978-1-55635-802-9

Manufactured in the U.S.A.

It is with deep gratefulness and love that I dedicate this book to the best home team there is—my wife, Kristin, and our three children, Jacob, Cooper, and Jillian.

Contents

Preface

What can you do to build a stronger team? How do you maximize the effectiveness and work ethic of your employees? How can you fight against a high turnover rate among those you oversee? Is a fragmented team keeping your organization from entering into new realms of success? There are foundational things you as a leader can put in place that will create and maintain productive and successful results in your work environment.

I am completely committed to the team concept in the workplace. Obviously, much more can be accomplished by a finely tuned team of people than can be accomplished by one person; but more than that, people thrive when they are in an environment that values a team approach to the task(s) at hand. Establishing and cultivating team dynamics in and among those you oversee will spark a fresh fire of productivity that will be as noticeable as it is enjoyable.

I want to share six principles that when consistently employed will build confidence among your staff and increase levels of productivity as you oversee, empower, and lead your team. These principles will apply across a broad spectrum of applications—executives, administrators, principals, coaches, managers, and pastors, to name a few—and will help you as a team leader to develop a team of people who are highly productive, strong, and unified.

Acknowledgments

I AM extremely fortunate to have been positively influenced by many people who have generously poured into my life. Time and words cannot list them all here, but I would be missing a moment of opportunity if I do not mention some of those who have spoken into my life on the importance of effective leadership—Dave Friese and Alan Hamilton, early mentors through my formative years. Thank you both for seeing potential in me early on and taking the time to mentor me. Mark Tatlock, who gave me opportunities to lead throughout my college years, thank you for the time spent building into my life at The Master's College. Chuck Swindoll, who has been a tremendous source of wisdom and encouragement, thanks for giving me opportunities to flourish under your leadership. Tyler Scott and Jeff Zabel—together we experienced friendship and teamwork at its best during our time together at Neighborhood Church of Castro Valley. And last but certainly not least, my father, Bruce Eldridge, thank you for the wisdom and encouragement you have brought (and still bring) to my life. Your example is the one I have always respected the most.

Acknowledgments

I would also like to thank several people who have given of their time to see this project to completion. A special thanks to my mother, Kathy Eldridge, who did much of the editing and "word smithing." Thanks for putting so much effort into making *TEAM* a reality. Thanks to Tabitha Teves, Mandy Koski, Butch Monk, and all those at Wipf and Stock for their help. Finally, I would like to thank the team I currently lead as of the writing of this book. Erin Vassey, Ryan Suzuki, Danny Strange, Joe Koski, Paul Keim, Tabitha Teves, and Dani Cromwell, thank you all for the incredible opportunity it has been to team up with each of you.

1

Why Team?

WHAT THE TEAM WANTS

EVERY ORGANIZATION wants to achieve the kind of success that leads to even greater success and every leader wants to guide a successful venture. Leaders with drive want to be surrounded by people who have an overarching desire to expand all boundaries and utilize their talents for the good of the goal. Effective team members see problems as challenges, boundaries as movable, and the synergism of the team as a way to reach their goals. It's important to note, however, that a group of people working towards a common goal will not necessarily make them a team. They might merely be "a group of people working towards a common goal."

The productive dynamic that a team possesses must be pursued with strong resolve and nurtured vigilantly. Finding the magical alchemy that turns a group of people into an effective team can make all the difference between what *can* be accomplished and what *will* be accomplished. An effective, cohesive team is a power to be reckoned with; not only do team members work with each other, they work alongside of each other to accomplish more together than they could alone. A team must own the belief that more will be accomplished together than individually.

Before we go into this discussion any further, let's consider some important definitions. Being productive and being successful are terms that are often used synonymously. This, however, should not be the case. One (success) identifies with an end result, while the other (productivity) identifies with a *process* that yields the end result.

Success

Success, in the purest sense of the word, is the achievement of something attempted. As a result, the measurement of success will be as different as the teams themselves and, though much can and has been written about success, the purpose of this book will be to focus on the importance of productivity. (Picture success as characterized by many different shades of color and productivity as simply described in black and white.)

There are times in the pursuit of success that the process (productivity) is underappreciated. Long-term success is ultimately determined by the strength of the production line. If productivity is inconsistent in any way, success will be equally inconsistent. So, with the desire to create the type of success that everyone really wants (long-term, stable, and so forth) let's focus our attention on the means to the end—productivity.

Productivity

Productivity is the action that leads to success. The measuring rod for success may vary from team to team, but the measuring rod for productivity is universal. Every team, no matter what they are seeking to accomplish, is either being productive or they are not. High productivity is the means to the end; highly productive teams focus their efforts intently on accomplishing the things that will bring success. Sometimes, productivity involves robots or computers, but even then, the human element is an integral part of the process.

Our focus in this book will be on the people who move the process forward—the productive people (producers) who accomplish the tasks that result in success. Leaders who focus solely on the end result (success) would do well to consider the importance of the process that leads to that result. Team leaders must learn to value the process, and more specifically, the people involved in the process. Leaders who do not value their teams ultimately do themselves and the people on their teams a great disservice.

> ONLY THE RIGHT PEOPLE DOING THE RIGHT JOB CAN CREATE THE RIGHT TEAM.

The emphasis of this book is to identify the essentials necessary to cultivate a strong team, keeping in mind that a strong team is first and foremost comprised of productive people. So, before we consider the core essentials of team, let's look at the criteria that can be used to identify an effective team member.

When I consider the various teams I have led or served on, the one thing that has consistently proven to be nonnegotiable is that you absolutely must have the right people doing the jobs that best fit their gifts and abilities. Whether you build a team from the ground up or inherit a team, a very keen eye must observe each team member to make sure he or she has high potential (proven or predicted) to be a producer. Only the right people doing the right job can create the right team.

HOW THE TEAM GETS THERE

The Right People

One of the keys to building a cohesive energized team is hiring and/or retaining productive people. Every person on a winning team must commit wholeheartedly to a high level of productivity. Nobody wants to face everyday tasks with the thought that success is unattainable. On the contrary, we want to walk into our offices and take on our challenges knowing with certainty that success is right around the corner. Most of the time, it's more than a few blocks away, but people with drive and desire have a way of making a marathon seem like an enjoyable walk in the park. Team members who are producers will stay actively engaged in the process; they will work hard and remain focused.

Most people are proficient enough at what they do that, if they choose, they can enter into a kind of mental cruise control for most of their day (often unbeknownst to their uplink). These are the drudges of your company and they are rarely in it for anything other than a paycheck. In fact, because of their penchant for idle chit-chat and highly distracting and unproductive work habits, they actually work against the efforts of true producers. This type of weak and uncommitted work ethic is demoralizing and destructive in any context, but most especially with regards to a team. Your team needs to feel that its efforts as a whole are being matched by each individual team member. Anything short of that will impede the forward progress you have worked hard to initiate.

Drive (an inner force that compels action towards a goal) and a robust, focused work ethic (doing what is required—and often more—whether or not anyone is watching) are two essential character traits of hardworking people. They are traits that are cultivated from within and over time are evidenced by a credible track record and high productivity. In other words, drive and a strong work ethic are the one-two punch of all great producers.

Producers are usually the first people at the office every day. They have a determined diplomacy in any situation, no matter the circumstances, and they are able to stay focused when others are preoccupied with situations that have become troublesome and tedious. A producer can discern between things that waste time and energy, and tasks that, though tedious and mundane, will yield necessary results. When producers sense other team members are becoming entangled with things that are pulling the team away from a goal, they can see a way through the situation and tactfully (yet firmly) refocus their teammates on the goal. In a very natural way, producers are able to make the best of every situation. You hand them lemons and they instinctively think lemonade.

> A PRODUCER CAN DISCERN BETWEEN THINGS THAT WASTE TIME AND ENERGY, AND TASKS THAT, THOUGH TEDIOUS AND MUNDANE, WILL YIELD NECESSARY RESULTS.

People like this are in high demand. You probably have a few of them in your ranks (perhaps quite a few). We're not talking about super-humans; we're talking about people who value the focus of every great team—high productivity. When you are able to bring together the right individuals doing the right jobs, you are on your way to success. Molding these *individuals* into a group of people who have the ability to focus and produce as a *team* will be the next step.

When teammates work together to achieve team goals, not only will they have a gratifying sense of accomplishment but the personal satisfaction of enjoying their work. Can you imagine leading a team of people who actually love their jobs? The people on your team want success as much as you do—they also want to enjoy their work. When people enjoy their work, they work harder and the ability to work hard is enhanced in a strong team environment. It follows then that when you create a strong team environment you will optimize the ability of your team to focus their efforts and experience success—together.

Team members need to know that the value of hard work is something the entire team is committed to. No one should have to worry about being the only person on the team who is expending effort. Effective teams are filled with members who trust that those around them are working every bit as hard as they are. And it is very easy to determine when this is the case.

Consider a crew team. The men or women rowing the boat truly have no way of knowing whether or not the people in back of them are pulling with everything they've got. Actually, it's also impossible to know if the people in front of them are doing any more than merely going through the motions. There is only one factor that can determine whether or not the entire crew is pulling to its full potential—speed. So it is with your team, with each goal achieved, your team begins a forward movement that is noticed by others. The air seems easier to breathe, the objective seems more achievable, success seems to come at an ever-increasing pace, and best of all, when your team members experience victory, they clearly will want more of it.

However, there is something that must not be overlooked. While it is true that productive people work hard, it is the synergy of your team that produces success. There must be a strong belief that the sum of the whole is greater than the sum of its parts—everyone working together with focus and energy accomplishes the goal. Sadly, few leaders actually understand that victory is only realized as a result of the efforts of the team. At the end of the day, accomplishment belongs to the group, not to the individuals who make up that group or the leader they follow. It is the result of everyone working together that accomplishes the goal.

I love it when a football coach states the obvious after a game by saying something like "Football games are won by football players." The game is not won by the coach (though he is crucial). It's not won by the fans (though they are important). The game is not won because of the equipment, the stadium, or the referees (though some bad calls have blown a few good games). No, the game itself is won or lost by the efforts of those on the field—the team; and so it will be with your team. The greatest possible success will be achieved as a result of team effort.

> WHILE IT IS TRUE THAT PRODUCTIVE PEOPLE WORK HARD, IT IS THE SYNERGY OF YOUR TEAM THAT PRODUCES SUCCESS.

We've talked about finding the right people for your team; now, let's talk about the elephant in the room that no one likes to talk about—the wrong people.

The Wrong People

The person on your team who is not making a significant enough contribution must be identified (keep in mind there may be more than one person). One of the marks of a good leader is the ability to recognize the strengths and weaknesses of the people on his team. I'm reminded of a past television show called "The Weakest Link."[1] It was a BBC creation that produced a game

1. The Weakest Link, http://en.wikipedia.org/wiki/The_Weakest_Link (accessed 13 Nov 2007).

show that brought unrelated people together to work as a team. Each segment of the show included a time when the team voted for the weakest contributor. The host would then chime in by humiliating and dismissing that person with the now famous phrase, "You are the weakest link. Goodbye!" As I watched the show I was shocked by the host's seeming lack of compassion for the weakest link and, at times, felt guilty because secretly I would have loved to dismiss certain people on my past teams in the same way. Suffice it to say, in the real world you can't dismiss the wrong people on your team with a curt "You are the weakest link. Goodbye!" But dismiss them you must or it will force other teammates to make up for the lost efforts of the weak link, which in turn will cause factions to exist and a subsequent breakdown of team cohesiveness.

When a leader identifies someone on the team who is not contributing enough, that leader must ask several questions including, but not limited to, those listed below.

1. Can this person (or these people) be salvaged?

2. Can I help to develop this person into someone whose life is marked by productivity and hard work?

3. Is this person a "bud" that needs water and sunshine (i.e., my time and resources) in order to blossom into something better?

4. Can I remove the invisible hurdles that will enable this person to work effectively with other team members?

If the answer is no to a majority of these questions, you must face the truth and act graciously, decisively, and immediately. You could spend two weeks lying awake at night trying to think of the best thing to say to this person, or simply have an honest, grace-filled conversation about the facts of the matter. Remember, in retaining someone who values other things, you could very well be keeping this person from being successful in another environment. An effective leader will always do what is best for the team as a whole, and though this is sometimes a very difficult thing to do, it *must* be done to ensure the cohesiveness of a team focused on success.

What about the wrong person who, given time and training, might become the right person? If you are considering retaining a team member because he has potential, you have another series of questions to answer and things to consider.

1. Will the time it takes to challenge this person to greater levels of personal drive and determination be worth your effort?

2. Will the diverting of resources needed to accomplish this be injurious to the efforts of the team?

3. Will team morale be negatively impacted as you spend energy and resources trying to pull the low achiever up to a level where he or she will be accepted as a contributing member of the team?

Let's suppose that you decide to take the challenge and work with this person. There will be times when your efforts are rewarded and you will be able to bring a person to a level of productivity that will allow him or her to become a contributing team member. There will be times, however, when as the team leader you must be willing to cut

> MORE IS AT STAKE ON A DYSFUNCTIONAL TEAM THAN BAD WORKING RELATIONSHIPS.

your losses for the good of the team. If you find yourself down the road a bit, second-guessing your decision, it is essential that you make a midcourse correction immediately. Remember, as you worked with the low achiever you can be sure that the rest of the team noticed the extra attention given to that person. So, if and when the time comes to move your weak link along, you must communicate your decision to the entire team—after the fact—and everyone must move on. (Discussion regarding details of your decision must be seen as counter productive and uncalled for.) When the wrong people are gone and the right people remain, you will find that your team will have a clearer focus and an energized commitment to each other and to the process.

WHAT THE TEAM NEEDS

Because great leaders focus on what it takes to stimulate a team dynamic, attention needs to be given (by the team leader) to the elements that cultivate a productive team. Establishing and maintaining a highly productive team is not without challenges. It demands much from both the leader and those on the team. More is at stake on a dysfunctional team than bad working relationships. The overall productivity of an organization will be greatly compromised when those doing the work aren't doing it with unified intent and cooperation. Leaders would do well to take notice that a finely tuned team will be their greatest asset. But what makes a team? What are the essentials needed for a group of productive people to become a team of producers? I believe there are six core essentials that when applied will cause the concept of team to take deep root in the lives of those you lead. They are:

Environment
Camaraderie
Respect
Purpose
Encouragement
Celebration

Each of these six essentials has equal importance in the development and preservation of a productive team. When utilized they will help you fan the flame of teamwork, ensure team success, and assist you as you build the type of team that will continue to attract the right people, as well as retain those you lead right now. Let's turn our attention to the essentials that exist in the life of a dynamic team.

2

Environment

THERE ARE two parts to every working environment that
are always active in the life of an organization. Both are
completely different, but serve the same purpose. There is a
physical environment, which is the actual workplace, and a
nonphysical environment, which is simply the atmosphere
that the team leader creates. In other words, environment
comprises both the look and the feel of the workplace and
these two elements are both important in the life of a team.
The feel of the environment is the more difficult of the two
for the team leader to create. The look of the environment
takes one (and only one) thing—money. We'll analyze the
look of the work environment in a moment but first let's
consider the feel of your work environment.

THE DUFFIELD EFFECT

In 2004, software giant *PeopleSoft*[1] was bought out by one of its top competitors. By the time this takeover was complete, *PeopleSoft* had run the course from being a start-up company with only a few employees and great vision, to becoming an industry giant valued at and purchased for more than ten billion dollars. Though the *PeopleSoft* product was well known throughout the world, there was another force at work within its ranks that was not as well known. In fact, unless you were close to the company and/or its employees, you might have missed it completely. On the outside, *PeopleSoft* might have appeared to be in line with every other company. Like its competitors, it was a billion-dollar empire that had a worldwide reputation. It had a dynamic leader (all great companies do) and was headquartered in the San Francisco Bay Area of Northern California, which has played host to a variety of successful computer software companies. There remained, however, a big difference between *PeopleSoft* and other large companies and this is what it was. While most companies only consider the "bottom line" to be the focal point of success, the leaders of *PeopleSoft* kept the process (and primarily the *people* involved in the process) at front and center.

> THOUGH ORGANIZATIONS MAY ACHIEVE THEIR GOALS WITHOUT CREATING A TEAM ENVIRONMENT, I CAN'T HELP BUT THINK OF WHAT THEY COULD BE ACCOMPLISHING IF THIS IMPORTANT PRINCIPLE OF TEAM EXISTED IN THEIR RANKS.

1. "Finally, Oracle to buy PeopleSoft," http://money.cnn.com/2004/12/13/technology/oracle_peoplesoft (accessed 14 Nov 2007).

David A. Duffield[2] (who was known and referred to as "DAD" around the office) knew the important role *feel* should play in a productive environment. Duffield created a winsome and healthy atmosphere where work was (obviously) accomplished yet done with ease and enjoyment. There were a variety of things that Duffield and his top leaders did to create a winsome and enjoyable environment for his team. He held regular rallies where the whole Pleasanton office came together to take part in a "pump-up" session that was reminiscent of homecoming weekend when you were in high school. He was rarely found around the office wearing a three thousand dollar suit but rather one of his trademark denim or Hawaiian shirts. Duffield spent one million dollars a year on bagels available everyday for *PeopleSoft* employees! *PeopleSoft* even had an in-house band (The Raging Dave's) that played at corporate events as well as special engagements held for members of the *PeopleSoft* team. Many things were true of *PeopleSoft* and one thing was absolutely certain—*PeopleSoft* was an amazing place to work.

Duffield could have built his company like a heavily guarded prison camp—no fun, strict rules, and the constant fear that "big brother" was watching. The *PeopleSoft* product would still have been successful and generated a healthy bottom line for employees and stockholders alike. However, I believe that the success *PeopleSoft* achieved would have been significantly reduced were it not for what I call "The Duffield Effect." At his core, David Duffield wanted the people who worked in his company to enjoy their jobs. Yes, they needed to be able to produce but he genuinely made it a goal to allow work to be accomplished in an environment where employees had fun along the way. Can you imagine!

2. "Restart: David Duffield 2.0, *PeopleSoft* founder is back in business," http://www.peoplesoft-planet.com/Dave-Duffield-Workday.html (accessed 14 Nov 2007).

Duffield successfully ushered "team" into his company by creating a *feel* in the environment that made work seem like a pleasant stroll on the beach. And for his efforts in creating an enjoyable atmosphere in which to work, Duffield was given something every leader wants—hardworking teammates who loved to go to work everyday. They got along with each other, worked exceptionally well together, and displayed high levels of productivity.

I have personally known several *PeopleSoft* employees. Each and every time that I have spoken with someone from the *PeopleSoft* team about his or her job the explanation would start in the exact same way—with a smile. It was as if in asking them about what they did they could not help but get mentally caught up in a good memory that was connected to their work at *PeopleSoft*. On the other hand, I've known many people who, when talking about their jobs with various companies, have always seemed stiff and overly serious—kind of like a kid reciting his lines in the school play. Though organizations may achieve their goals without creating a team environment, I can't help but think of what they could be accomplishing if this important principle of team existed in their ranks.

The Duffield Effect takes place when a normal working environment is turned into an enjoyable and dynamic place in which hard work is accomplished *and* a team is woven together. Remember, more will be accomplished when people work together than when they work alone and the *feel* of your environment will affect the success of your team. A strong and healthy work environment will not only allow your team members to enjoy their work, it will also stimulate them to work harder to accomplish the purposes of your organization.

An effective team cannot exist (or continue to exist) without a healthy environment in which the concept of team is deeply rooted. If the people you lead feel that you are waiting for them to make a mistake so you can hand them walking papers, you are missing a big component in creating a highly productive team. Take the proverbial clipboard-toting roamer-of-the-halls and replace him with a healthy, enjoyable yet controlled feeling in the workplace that commands productivity and cultivates teamwork. The *feel* of the work environment is crucial and though an invisible entity, it is as obvious as sunshine on a clear day.

The other crucial element in a synergetic environment is the *physical space* where the work is accomplished. I call it the hub. I like to think of the hub in any given work environment as a very important focal point of the activity in the office—the locus of energy in the workplace. Your hub is the place where the most amount of work is done to accomplish the goals of your team. Regardless of where that place is, it should ultimately encourage a team dynamic. Though it is one of the most overlooked components of a successful team, the physical setting where work is accomplished is essential in building an effective team. Very few people have understood this better and displayed this more consistently over the past several years than the Maverick from Dallas, Texas, Mark Cuban[3].

THOUGH IT IS ONE OF THE MOST OVER-LOOKED COMPONENTS OF A SUCCESSFUL TEAM, THE PHYSICAL SETTING WHERE WORK IS AC-COMPLISHED IS ESSEN-TIAL IN BUILDING AN EFFECTIVE TEAM.

THE CUBAN CONCEPT

You have to *spend* money to *make* money. Most everyone agrees with this principle but not everyone follows through with it. Mark Cuban, owner of the Dallas Mavericks, not only under-

3. Mark Cuban, http://en.wikipedia.org/wiki/Mark_Cuban (accessed 14 Nov 2007).

stands this principle but he has rewritten the book on the overall effectiveness that it can produce. After selling *Broadcast.com* (an Internet product that led the market in streaming video) to Internet giant, *Yahoo!,* for several billions of dollars, Cuban took a part of his share of the sale proceeds and bought the Dallas Mavericks basketball team. Up to that point, the Mavericks had suffered through many years of disappointment and loss. Things were about to change dramatically.

Cuban made it abundantly clear that he was willing to spend whatever was needed to ensure a high amount of interest from fans and success from the team. He created a theme park-like environment at every game that felt more like a party than a basketball competition. Cuban spent money on his players. He invested in them by paying healthy salaries. He also invested heavily in improving areas that had heretofore suffered from lack of attention, such as a pristine weight room, locker room, and ultimately a new arena (the American Airlines Center). As a result, the Dallas Mavericks have been able to reinvent themselves as a true threat in the National Basketball Association. Cuban, who has got to be one of the most fun owners to ever own any franchise, spent his money creating a dynamic environment (look and feel) in which his team could accomplish its goals. The payday for his efforts was a trip to the playoffs in his first full year as owner and several others since then—oh, and millions of fans! The players do the winning but the environment helps to streamline their efforts and, as a result, brings productivity to the organization.

> AS THE TEAM LEADER, YOU MUST CONSCIOUSLY MAKE THE DECISION TO BUILD YOUR TEAM UP BY SUPPLYING THEM WITH THE THINGS THAT GIVE THEM THE BEST SHOT AT BEING PRODUCTIVE.

As an owner, Mark Cuban could have done whatever he wanted with the team—up to and including nothing at all. He could have had a great seat at every game and reaped the financial benefits of ownership (as even the worst teams can draw a crowd) but he is too good of a leader to be satisfied with the status quo. By paying attention to what his team needed, he set in place the necessary elements that would ultimately give his team the best chance for success. I call it "The Cuban Concept," and when it is applied, the table is set for high achievement.

As the team leader, you must consciously make the decision to build your team up by supplying them with the things that give them the best shot at being productive. Okay, so you don't have a billion dollars. Can you create a better physical environment in which your team can thrive? Yes! It will not be free but the good things in life rarely are. You must see it as an investment that will pay dividends in team morale and productivity and be fully worth your effort! If you want a team, you have to give them a home court. Where is your hub? In your particular situation, where is the most work done to create success for your organization? Wherever it is, you need to realize that the quality of the work that comes out of your hub will be directly affected by the quality of the working environment. The Cuban Concept simply demands that you give your team the things they need to be successful.

Sometimes that means putting a few paintings on the wall or buying new computers; other times it may mean moving office centers to a larger, more dynamic area. You can usually tell just by looking at the boardroom of an organization if it's a productive or nonproductive place. Great work is created in a great environment. This is the essence of The Cuban Concept.

The look and feel of your environment is critical to the goal of creating a highly productive team. Remember, as a leader you need to look at the environment where work is accomplished as an important element that will ultimately affect, positively or negatively, the cohesiveness of your team. Is it a fun atmosphere or a rigid one? Do people smile as they work or do they look like they are suffering? Do they regularly engage each other in healthy ways or are they too afraid that it will look like they are wasting company time? Are your people being asked to work as professionals in an amateur environment?

Paying keen attention to this element of team is often overlooked. However, I firmly believe that, based on clear evidence proving it to be so, you will create a stronger and deeper team if the office environment (look and feel) is not neglected. Good leaders need to be willing to do whatever is necessary to ensure the team's working environment has both the look and the feel of a place where a great team comes together to work hard everyday.

Each year when my department heads fill out a brief questionnaire (see Appendix A—Strategies and Goals Worksheet 2009) telling me about their strategic plans for the coming year, they conclude their report by answering one final question: "If you could have any 'wish list' item that would be helpful in bringing departmental success, what would it be and how would it help?" More times than not, their answers have something to do with the work environment. I give them permission to speak into the needs they have *and* offer solutions—and man alive do they know how to dream! Now,

> THEIR WORK AND THEIR PEOPLE ARE *THEIR* FOCUS; WHAT THEY NEED IN ORDER TO BE SUCCESSFUL IS *MINE*.

if I can accommodate any or all of their wishes, I do. Their work and their people are *their* focus; what they need in order to be successful is *mine*. The leader is responsible for creating the look and the feel of an environment that not only allows work to be accomplished but also encourages the cultivation and maintenance of a healthy team. Before you move on to the next essential in creating an effective team, consider how you can begin (or continue) to bring "The Duffield Effect" and/or "The Cuban Concept" into your team environment.

3

Camaraderie

I N THE previous chapter, we established that it takes deter-mination and dedication on the part of the team leader to create and maintain the look and feel of a team-friendly environment. The next step in developing a successful team is to cultivate an atmosphere of authentic concern for your team members. As you model genuine concern for them as individuals, they will find it easier to show this type of re-spect and regard for fellow teammates. It is absolutely criti-cal as you assemble the right people doing the right jobs in the right environment to infuse your team with the belief that teammates don't just work together—teammates are comrades.

GETTING ON THE SAME PAGE

The true potential for incredible success can be undermined when a team doesn't work well together. Even if the environment has the right look and feel, the concept of team is impossible to implement without genuine mutual concern among team members. A certain intangible chemistry needs to exist between teammates.

The first step in building camaraderie on your team goes back to our earlier discussion regarding the hiring process. As you are in the process of hiring people who will be a part of your team, you must remain cognizant as to whether or not they will add to or take away from the overall dynamic of your team. A major component of that dynamic will simply come down to personality. Yes, those on your team can maintain their individuality, but if you determine a particular personality is one that will clash with many on your team, do your team an early favor and politely pass from adding that person to your ranks. Do not hire people who cannot work well with others.

> **DO NOT HIRE PEOPLE WHO CANNOT WORK WELL WITH OTHERS.**

I have made it a habit to only hire and/or retain people on my team who not only work well *with* others, but can work hard *for* their teammates when the need arises. I am constantly monitoring the health level of team relationships, primarily in the professional setting, but sometimes in personal settings as well. I do my best to create venues for my team to grow closer with each other on a personal level so that they will not see each other as mere robots on an assembly line, but as comrades. I have a weekly lunch with my team (my treat), where we simply enjoy an hour together catching up with each other. Often, I'll purchase copies of a good leadership book I've recently read and give it to them as free reading and fodder for good dialog at our lunches.

My wife and I make time to have my team and their families over to our home. A great example of this happens on

Monday nights in the fall, when we have various staff members and their spouses spend time with us and each other in the relaxed atmosphere of our home. Nothing builds good camaraderie like dinner and a football game! Even though not everyone on my team is overly excited about football, they all have a great time talking about things that have nothing to do with their work. These nights are filled with little breakout conversations, enthusiastic cheering for great plays, casual eating together, and best of all, a deepening relationship that is cultivated between each of them (and their families). And it is that depth in their relationships that allows them to look past shortcomings (i.e., an unkind word that is exchanged in a moment of frustration).

Those moments when camaraderie is built between your team members become pivotal to the strength of your team when people don't feel like going forward anymore. If all that your employees have is their work, you'll be looking to fill an empty desk or two in a matter of time. Your team members must not only have their work but the feeling of camaraderie with their fellow teammates. Granted, you

> WHEN YOUR TEAM MEMBERS EXPERIENCE CAMARADERIE, THEY WILL WORK HARDER TO ENSURE TEAM SUCCESS.

might not enjoy football or having people over to your house—that's okay. The point is, never underestimate the value of time spent together both at and away from the hub.

I'm not advocating that everyone in your workplace must be the best of friends or that they go out to dinner with each other on a regular basis (though that would be a good thing). I'm talking about a relationship that goes deeper than what common courtesy demands. Making the quantum leap from being indifferent to actually caring about the people you work with is a vital move that allows for a better, sharper, and more effective team.

You might have no problem when it comes to making friends and/or finding people who share concern for your life but the people around you might not be so fortunate. As the team leader, you need to think of ways to allow for personal interactions to occur among your staff. As a result of attempting to build character traits such as loyalty, trust, and mutual respect into the individuals who comprise your team (remember, you must model these traits), positive connections will be made that will ultimately enhance the team dynamic.

If you cultivate a work environment where a life essential can occur (i.e., meaningful relationships), you will build into the personal and professional lives of your team and they will see and appreciate your efforts as a unique and enjoyable part of working for you. And if people enjoy working for you, they will not leave you. Moreover, when your team members experience camaraderie, they will work harder to ensure team success. In essence, by knocking down walls and building up relationships, you will pave the way for your organization to be filled with hardworking teammates who "hit it out of the park" *with* and *for* each other.

A CHANGE OF SCENERY

In the professional realm, besides our weekly lunches, our team also goes on two off-site retreats each year; one of them occurs in May. Summer is a busy time for our team, so a presummer retreat for refreshment and focus is always beneficial. About a month before the retreat, I purchase a leadership book for them to browse through in order to stimulate casual conversations during the retreat. We typically go to a comfortable place and invite a speaker who challenges us in various parts of our lives personally as well as collectively as a team. While a speaker might not be the right fit for your team, a casual atmosphere where camaraderie is cultivated in an enjoyable, nonworking environment goes a long way in building relationships on any team.

The other retreat is in late fall and primarily serves the purpose of allowing each department head to share his or her strategic goals for the coming year. Prior to this retreat, each of them fills out a brief questionnaire that works as a tool to narrow their goals into a tight focus (see Appendix A—Strategies and Goals Worksheet 2009). I meet with each person to discuss his or her goals and strategic plans for the coming year, my intention being to guide the individual strategies and goals as they relate to the "big picture" of what we will focus on accomplishing as a team. The Fall retreat then becomes a time when the entire team comes into an understanding of how the individual

> LIKE A LOYAL PLATOON OF SOLDIERS THAT LOOKS OUT FOR EACH OTHER IN THE HEAT OF THE BATTLE, SO A GOOD TEAM WILL LOOK TO PROTECT, ENHANCE, AND PRAISE THE WORK OF TEAMMATES.

goals will work synergistically to accomplish the overall goals of the team. This, in turn, allows "buy-in" and a sense of camaraderie as the team understands how each member will contribute to the success of the team as a whole. To ensure a healthy and productive time together, I start each of the meetings with the charge to "save the sarcasm" that might otherwise distract or inhibit the free flow of ideas. This time is very important for the productivity of our team and we take each person's strategy very seriously.

Like a loyal platoon of soldiers that looks out for each other in the heat of the battle, so a good team will look to protect, enhance, and praise the work of teammates. I make it my goal to be sure that each of my department heads is able to answer crucial questions not only about his or her department but also about the other departments represented on the team. This becomes easier as we spend time together, sharing goals and ideas in a healthy, productive atmosphere. Conversely, I can guarantee you that this will not happen as effectively if your team does not have a strong sense of camaraderie built into its DNA.

BRINGING BACK LONGEVITY

One of the problems with building camaraderie among your teammates is that when one of them leaves the team, the whole team feels the weight of the loss. Staff turnover is never enjoyable. It not only means filling another's shoes, but doing it with someone new to the team (which is particularly difficult if your team has been together for a long time). Once again, hiring the *right* person to take the place of another is a very important element in building an effective team; so, take the responsibility seriously and hire thoughtfully. No one likes to lose key members of his or her team; perhaps the following system of thought will make it a little easier to endure.

Though it is always difficult to lose good people, I have to remind myself that there is a reason why other opportunities have presented themselves to the departing team member—he is great at what he does, everything she touches turns to gold! And just as we lure good people from other places, our best team members will someday be lured away by someone else. Don't be concerned with the fact that the best people on your team may be courted by other companies who offer them "the world on a string." Instead, be concerned about those people in your ranks who never have another offer come their way.

You can be proactive in helping the members of your team make the decision to stay with you long before other opportunities arise. Salaries are a big part of that, as are opportunities for upward mobility. However, I believe that people walk away from their jobs permanently (jobs that offer good salaries and upward mobility) because they simply have not connected in a meaningful way with the people they spend the majority of their time with. If you build camaraderie among your people, they will have a very difficult time leaving your team.

Longevity is a term that is used to describe people who have been with an organization for a long period of time. Take a moment and think about those in your ranks who have achieved longevity. Are there many of them? If there are, I'm willing to wager they have established great relationships with others in the organization. You see, longevity and camaraderie are linked. The action point for you as a leader is to look for ways to create the latter without having to wait for the former.

If you have people in your company who have said "no" to outside opportunities because they believe in their work and that there is no replacing the joy of working with their team, find a way to move them into a more important role in your organization. Even if you can't promote them, give them some extra team responsibilities. You want these people to know you notice their contribution. Praise them in front of the team. Positively reinforce the fact that they are valued and you appreciate them. When people on the team start doing what

> IF YOU BUILD CAMA-
> RADERIE AMONG YOUR
> PEOPLE, THEY WILL
> HAVE A VERY DIFFICULT
> TIME LEAVING YOUR
> TEAM.

usually falls on the shoulders of the leader, you will know that your team is starting to function as a team. They are buying into the value of the team—don't miss the opportunity to capitalize on that. Once again, if you build a team that values camaraderie you will give yourself the opportunity for a low turnover rate among your staff.

FREEDOM TO FAIL

Keep in mind two simple concepts: 1) your team is more productive when they work together as a team and 2) the concept of team disintegrates when it is missing the critical element of camaraderie. If your team is productive, you will (or perhaps already have) come up against many challenges along the way. Camaraderie is paramount in dealing with and moving past these challenges.

I love to snow ski. My parents made it a point to have an annual winter vacation with our family at one of California's premier ski resorts. I remember ski school very early on in life. It was a time when gravity knew more about skiing than I did, so I was extremely grateful for the bales of hay that stood as barriers to a wayward "downhiller" like me. Maybe it was my early run-ins with the hay bales that allowed me to be unafraid of falling, but that fear (to a degree) was gone from nearly the beginning. Such is not the case with others I have seen on the ski slopes. I often see people going very slowly, panting like an Olympic sprinter, on a *bunny slope,* because of their gripping fear of falling. I bought a pin at this particular ski resort one year; it simply read "If you're not falling, you're not working!" Snow skiers miss out on the best parts of a mountain because they are paralyzed by the thought of falling (and I'm not talking about falling off a twenty-foot cliff, just falling down in general).

Great companies along with their great leaders have all shared this in common—they have all taken a fall once or twice. They understand a skier's principle that transcends the slopes and finds its way into the boardroom. If you're not falling, you're not working. And when those tough times come, nothing will get you through them cleaner and easier than a team of people who are committed to each other as much as they are to the goal.

They will simply dust each other off and get back to work—with and for each other.

As an aside, it behooves all leaders to create an atmosphere where the "freedom to fail" concept has some room to breathe. That is, your team should know that not all failures are unacceptable. You want your team to make good choices that directly relate to the integrity and forward progress of your organization, but you also need to encourage the type of decision making that generates out-of-the-box action points. Often, the removal of fear of failure will bring the greatest forms of creativity, and if you want your organization to stand out among those around you, you need to be more creative than they are. Trial and error is okay as long as the calculated risk isn't overly ridiculous. When your team comes across an error, you can salvage the situation (to a degree) by using that bump as an opportunity to create feelings of camaraderie. Pull the team together, discuss why the idea fell apart, encourage the person (or people) who have taken the hardest hit, dust them off, and get back to it! If you do this, you will have taken a presumably bad situation and turned it into a good one by creating the type of camaraderie that can only come about through enduring a tough situation together. A by-product of this type of reaction is that *your* personal stock will soar in the eyes of your team.

> GREAT COMPANIES ALONG WITH THEIR GREAT LEADERS HAVE ALL SHARED THIS IN COMMON—THEY HAVE ALL TAKEN A FALL ONCE OR TWICE.

Camaraderie is essential because it feeds a particular hunger of human nature. That hunger is called "community"—the strong need to affiliate—and your team wants it. If you are steering clear of building community in your organization among your staff, you are choosing to stay on the bunny slopes when the rest of the mountain is calling your name. When you allow your team the opportunity to connect on a meaningful level both at and away from the hub, you will multiply the efforts of your team by showing each member that he or she is valued.

If camaraderie builds up your team, mutual respect will keep it strong. This is the next essential in building and maintaining a highly productive team.

4

Respect

NOTHING WILL fragment a team faster than the absence of mutual respect. Highly productive teams are filled with people who work as hard at being respectable as they do at respecting those around them. If mutual respect is not demonstrated from every angle, the health of the team is, at best, superficial and, at worst, on the edge of meltdown. Have you ever met anyone who enjoys experiencing any form of condescension? Nobody likes to feel small and trivialized—especially on a team. It is the job of each team member to guard against being condescending or degrading to another, and to vigorously protect fellow teammates from the same things.

LOOKING OUT FOR EACH OTHER

I have always had a deep appreciation for the military. Our country owes a tremendous debt of gratitude to the men and women who serve all of us by being willing to protect the freedoms we enjoy everyday. My brother-in-law, Travis, served a six-year term in the United States Marine Corps as an embassy guard in Turkey, Israel, and Greece. I always enjoyed connecting with Travis because it was fun to live vicariously through his action-packed life. Military personnel, like Travis, understand the principle of respect better than most. When a high-ranking officer steps onto the floor, it's heels together and chest out! The respect one soldier gives to another of higher rank is decidedly different, however, than what must be observed around your office.

The nature of military respect is based on rank, and rank alone. Granted, there are times when ranking military personnel will show respect to lower ranking soldiers because of work ethic and/or bravery. It is also true that there are times when lower ranking officers will only respect an authority above them while that authority is in their presence, which really isn't respect at all. Regardless of what is going on in the mind of the soldier (rank not withstanding), military respect is an integral part of the order and discipline needed to produce the finely-tuned, effective organization that is the United States military.

> NOTHING WILL FRAGMENT A TEAM FASTER THAN THE ABSENCE OF MUTUAL RESPECT.

The respect that is necessary between those serving together on your team goes far deeper than simple rank or forced respect. I'm not advocating that you drop your organization chart into the garbage. No, you need the organizational component because it is very important in keeping the team focused. However, if your managers, directors, and/or other middle or upper management people are *only* respected because of their position, your team is in the danger zone. Effective teammates make it their intention to respect each other at all times and guard their fellow teammates from a lack of respect from anyone else. I have made it a habit to not engage in conversations (in a critical way) with anyone about another member of my team unless that other teammate is right there with us.

One summer, I was on a retreat in Palm Springs, California, and my wife and I were having dinner with a few friends. In the course of the conversation, I told a story about a few of the guys who worked for me. I was completely unaware that one of the people we were having dinner with was upset with these guys from my office because of a misunderstanding of some kind. It was as if a floodgate opened at the table when one of the men we were eating with began to launch verbal arrows at these team members of mine (who weren't present). He got a few sentences into his rant before I very kindly interrupted and said, "I can tell that you're a little upset at these guys. I've got to tell you, though, I try to keep it real with my team, and I really think we should postpone this conversation until those guys can be with us." He understood and we changed the conversation to lighter, more enjoyable topics.

On our way back to our hotel, my wife Kristin said, "No wonder your team loves you!" The bottom line is that we all love it when someone sticks up for us. I know, beyond a shadow of a doubt, that my team would have done the same for me—so I owe it to them to keep their respectability high. In that particular case, I called both of the men in question into my office the first day I got back and got a clearer picture of the issue, which led to an almost immediate resolution. I was so glad that I gave them the benefit of the doubt, as it proved to be a real moment of teambuilding when they clearly saw me in their corner, guarding them when they were not around.

The basis for the respect that should permeate your team ought to center on the fact that they *serve on the same team.* Slander, gossip, and biting words will fragment and, in turn, ruin your team more quickly than any other thing. It is really nothing more than common courtesy to show respect for another. The end of common courtesy is often caused by a certain level of familiarity, not unlike the familiarity that a family might enjoy. Growing up, would you say you demonstrated a high level of respect for your siblings? Probably not (though, maybe you were an anomaly). That high level of respect probably existed in some form, but demonstrating it seemed pointless because of your very close ties to each other. Let me ask you another question. When people started making fun of your siblings, did you stand still and let it happen? You probably did not. At that point, familiarity kicked into a realm where normally it would not go; when they weren't around to stand up for themselves, you became "the great enforcer of respect" for your family.

> WHEN YOUR TEAM MEMBERS LEARN TO RESPECT EACH OTHER, THEY WILL BEGIN TO HAVE MORE RESPECT FOR OTHER TEAMS IN YOUR ORGANIZATION.

Great teams know each other very well, especially if camaraderie is developing. Don't let familiarity breed complacency when it comes to respect. The spirit of camaraderie that your team members have with each other will be a tremendous springboard for the mutual respect that should exist between them. While it is important to protect the respectability of your teammates when they are not present, it is particularly important to demonstrate respect for your teammates as they work in your hub. Remember, everyone on your team is important in accomplishing your goals. If someone feels that they have no place on your team (for lack of respect), you will pay dearly in lack of productivity. However, when your teammates know that they have the respect of those around them, they will work harder and more effectively—respect serving as fuel for their fire. Furthermore, you will soon find that mutual respect among your team members will have a domino effect. When your team members learn to respect each other, they will begin to have more respect for other teams in your organization.

DEALING WITH DISRESPECT

When I sense there is a lack-of-respect issue looming around our office, I'm quick to get to the bottom of it, as it tends to be a disease that festers and quickly spreads, if not dealt with immediately and decisively. I simply pull the person in question into my office and open the door for conversation. I'll ask how things are going between them and their teammates. I'll do whatever I can to get that person to talk about what is frustrating him and why he is not respecting those around him. Usually, if done sensitively, the truth comes out and I am able to validate his frustrations and call him to something that is imperative in the life of every great team—short-term memory loss—the matter has been dealt with, now move forward.

The people around you will disappoint you (and more particularly, their teammates) at some point or another. Once you have worked the situation through with them, you need to challenge them to get past it, let it go, and refocus on mutual team respect. Most of the time, just talking about things helps relieve existing tension. As obvious as it seems, you must remember that you are not working with robots; you are working with people and they have feelings. Everyone wants to be respected, and while individuals can't do anything to force the respect of others, they have total control over the respect they give to others.

More than anything else, however, your team must respect you, the leader. Teams that don't have a high level of respect for their leaders are headed for turbulent times. Of course, it bears repeating you need to maintain a high level of respectability, but when you see a lack of respect from one or a few of your team members aimed at you, drop everything and get to the bottom of it. Sometimes it's a small matter that a little humility can quickly clear up. At other times, it's a "biggie" that needs gentle wisdom to resolve. Your efforts will be rewarded and you will actually gain ground by showing your team members that you value their input and feelings.

If you set up a meeting with someone who is displaying a lack of respect for you and/or fellow teammates and the trend continues on into and past that meeting, you have a tough call to make. A friend of mine led an office where one of his office staff could not work together with the rest of the team and it seemed to clearly stem from her inability to respect her teammates. She was a woman who came to work with the proverbial chip on her shoulder and seemed to desire nothing more than to do what was required of her, collect her paycheck, and leave. As I listened to his story, it was clear to me that she was sour and everything that came out of her mouth about her teammates, especially their leader, was sour. He noticed her interactions with those she was supposed to be supporting were often cutting and short. It was killing the positive feel of the environment and breaking down the team. My friend took the high road and tried to discover if there were issues behind the scenes that were frustrating this assistant. He told me that as hard as he tried to get to the bottom of the issues, in the end, he (correctly) discerned that the true problem was her attitude. She, very simply, did not respect those around her. When it was clear that no change was forthcoming, even after his attempts to gather her in, he had to let her go. After she was gone, my friend told me, "It was as though the clouds were lifted and a new day had come! All of the sudden the road block was gone and the team hit new levels of enjoyment and productivity." This happened because mutual respect had been rediscovered among teammates. Perhaps it needs to be rediscovered on your team.

A BIG PIECE OF THE PUZZLE

Hopefully, you won't have to release anyone to reinstate mutual respect on your team. If your team is having respect issues, they might be resolved with one conversation—and that would be the best conversation of your week! When your team taps into the importance of mutual respect, the quality of their working relationships will increase as quickly as their productivity. If you have hired sharp people, they will know the difference between forced respect (like in the military) and genuine respect.

Respect for others is a quality that a person develops internally and expresses externally. Many people are good at the latter without working on the former. If you only have people on your team who are gratuitous with each other, pasting on smiles, and *showing* respect but not *being* respectful, you've got nothing more than smoke and mirrors. Respect is a crucial element in the lives of your team members individually, and will

> YOU HAVE TO BE *KNOWN* TO BE *RESPECTED*. YOU HAVE TO BE *RESPECTED* TO BE *TRUSTED*. YOU HAVE TO BE *TRUSTED* TO BE *FOLLOWED*. AND YOU HAVE TO BE *FOLLOWED* TO BE A *LEADER*.

work as a building block in productively moving them forward as a team. This type of quality needs to be modeled—and in case you've forgotten, you're the model.

Here is a little saying I use frequently: "You have to be *known* to be *respected*. You have to be *respected* to be *trusted*. You have to be *trusted* to be *followed*. And you have to be *followed* to be a *leader*." The quest of becoming *known* is what camaraderie is all about. Once that is in place, respect will follow and it is crucial—both to your team and to you as the leader—if trust is to develop. Respect and trust are connected, and trust is essential if you expect to have others follow you. Do the members of your team have each other's backs? Do they have yours? Perhaps more importantly, do you have theirs? Remember, building mutual respect is not just about making sure your team respects you, it is equally as important that you respect each member of your team and that they respect each other.

Keep the pattern in mind: Known—Respected—Trusted—Followed.

As the leader, you must never minimize the value of respect. Highly productive teams are professional on all levels. Pettiness (the fuel for a lack of respect) and petty people who disrespect fellow teammates should have no place on your team. If your team is missing the ingredient of respect, take the needed time to consider how you can share the importance of it with your team. Start by modeling it and then make the development of mutual respect a team priority. You will be rewarded with a highly effective team of people who enjoy working together toward common goals.

5

Purpose

GREAT LEADERS keep the purpose of their organization in crystal clear focus every single day. When the purpose of the organization is out of focus, energies will be scattered instead of streamlined, causing feelings of frustration, as well as lack of fulfillment among the individual members of the team. Each member must feel he or she has purpose (personally) in the endeavors of the team and the team must understand (collectively) what their overarching purpose is. In other words, your team always needs to keep an eye on the big picture.

WHO AM I AND WHY AM I HERE?

One of my favorite moments of any football game is when the respective teams take the field. If you've ever been to a professional football game, I'm sure you remember the scene. There is, most often, a fair amount of hype built into the crowd—loud music, cheerleaders, floating blimps that shoot out confetti, and mascots that coax the crowd to jump to their feet and make more noise. It is controlled chaos at its finest. All the while, the team is in the tunnel getting ready to come out and play the game. During those pregame moments of euphoria, what do you think the football teams are thinking about? I can promise you that the best teams are focused and intent on one thing—doing what they need to do to win the game. Sure, they have families to worry about, investments to consider, contracts to negotiate, and other extraneous things that could be running up their mental tab. But the very best players choose to set those thoughts aside. Great teams choose to leave everything in the locker room *except for the game;* everything and everyone else becomes secondary to the overall purpose of the team. By the time those moments arrive in the tunnel the coaches have so focused the attention of their teams that their purpose is crystal clear. When those players take the field, they have one thing on their minds—victory.

> ARE YOUR PEOPLE "TAKING THE FIELD" WITH NO CLUE AS TO WHAT THEIR PURPOSE IS AND WHAT THEY ARE RESPONSIBLE FOR AS IT PERTAINS TO ACCOMPLISHING THAT PURPOSE?

Can you imagine the bedlam that would ensue if a football team did not know what its purpose was? Imagine a stadium tunnel that somehow was able to give amnesia to each player and coach as they broke through the damp darkness onto the light of the field. Players and coaches would be running all over the place, some to get water, others to see what the people close by were yelling about. Some would go to the other sideline to inquire about the different colors of the opposing team's uniforms; others might just turn around and walk back up the tunnel. A few might make it to their sideline, but then would have no idea what to do once they got there. Because no one could remember their purpose as a team or how they would personally be used to accomplish that purpose, defeat would be assured.

That seems a silly scenario, I know, but sadly, lack of purpose and the resulting aimless chaos is a reality for many teams. Are your people "taking the field" with no clue as to what their purpose is and what they are responsible for as it pertains to accomplishing that purpose? Here is the big question. Can you explain, in fifteen words or less, what the purpose of your team is? Take a moment and try. Look away from this book and come up with your best purpose statement—remember no more than fifteen words. In fact, here are three free words that won't count in your fifteen, "We exist to . . ."

Could you do it? Most cannot and those who can are rarely surrounded by others who can do the same. This might seem like a small thing but it is not. The productivity of your team is paying a huge price for a lack of clearly articulated purpose. Once again, it is your job as the team leader to know and clearly state the purpose of your organization as often as necessary— you simply cannot overstate it. Everyone should know what the purpose of the team is in order to give 100 percent effort to seeing that purpose accomplished.

SETTING GOALS

Depending on the goals that are in place, true success will be measured differently across teams. Sports teams want victories and championships, broadcasting networks want viewers or a listening audience, financial institutions want investors, universities want high academic marks, ministers want transforming impact, corporations want market share, car dealers want to move inventory, the list is as endless as it is diverse. Your vision will be different than other leaders—that is the beauty of creativity and diversity. However, one thing is common among leaders who successfully cast vision for the people they lead, when working to achieve a goal, whatever it might be, *team* is paramount. The organizational purpose statement of your team must communicate compelling vision and your goals must act as a clear roadmap to accomplishing that vision.

This process of stating purpose and setting goals is critical to your success as a team. It involves both why you are doing what you are doing (purpose) and how you will accomplish your stated purpose (goals). All goals must reflect the overall purpose of the team and that of the organization in which the team functions.

Once goals have been set, effective leaders must work to keep a close watch on those who are working to accomplish the purpose of the organization. To this end, you must learn to differentiate between down time and dead time. Down time usually involves a period of time or a season in which your team is not as busy. Dead time is simply wasted time. Don't worry about the former but be concerned about the latter.

Dead time around the hub is often due to a lack of clear organizational purpose combined with a lack of accountability between teammates as they work on goals that will bring that purpose about. Reducing dead time around your office may be as simple as making sure your team knows what they should be doing. You know what your purpose is (unless you still haven't figured out your fifteen-word purpose statement). Have you shared it with your team? Have you been assuming that they know what it is? Even your sharpest people might be a little confused as to what their purpose is. It would serve you well, as the leader, to have a meeting in which you express—perhaps, once again—what the purpose of the team is. You will focus the work energy of your team and simultaneously reduce dead time around your hub. When the purpose is clarified, everyone will have a greater understanding of how individual goals line up with overall purpose.

When I have my team work on their strategic goals for the coming year, I first ask them to state in fifteen words or less, four top-tier goals that they will seek to accomplish in their departments. There is nothing magical about stating your organizational purpose in fifteen words or less as compared to twenty words or any other number. The point is to be succinct yet thorough; too many words in goal setting, as

> REDUCING DEAD TIME AROUND YOUR OFFICE MAY BE AS SIMPLE AS MAKING SURE YOUR TEAM KNOWS WHAT THEY SHOULD BE DOING.

well as in purpose statements, make them difficult to grasp at a glance. When you limit your words, you force yourself to be concise. My challenge to the team is to thoughtfully consider what they intend to accomplish, and communicate that clearly.

The second question I ask them is to expand on each of their four goals, giving clarity as to how each will be accomplished. The third question asks them to connect the dots between their goals and the overarching purpose of our team. Did you catch that? The third question might seem small to you, but I consider it to be a fish-or-cut-bait moment for their expressed goals. If they cannot show me how their departmental goals will ultimately coincide with the overall purpose of the team, some retooling must take place. All of the efforts of each member must be motivated by the overall purpose of the team. Everyone must work together with that purpose in mind or efforts will be wasted and your team will fragment faster than an amnesia-stricken football team.

A clearly articulated purpose not only streamlines efforts, it serves as a great accountability tool. It is so much easier to gauge the productivity of your team if you know what the team is supposed to be doing. My teammates know what it is that they are supposed to be accomplishing. They also know that I know what their goals are. If they start to get off course, it is very easy to remind them of what they have expressed as their goals. It is not me telling them what to do. Rather, I am reminding them of what they said they wanted to do.

Occasionally, a mid-season idea is created by one of my teammates. Whenever someone comes to my office with such an idea, I weigh it against our purpose statement. If it lines up to our purpose, we may choose to move forward with it. If it does not (support our purpose), it flatlines then and there. Only the things that accomplish our expressed purpose (or purposes) get the privilege of our attention, everything else is jettisoned.

EVERYONE MATTERS

The individual goals of your team members will directly affect the overall success of your team. Each member must understand what he or she is contributing to the team and (if you work with a large company) to the organization as a whole. People want to belong; they want to identify themselves with things they care about. Our culture is seeing a major shift in the reasons why someone takes a position at any given company. It is no longer enough for people to take jobs that pay well. Those who do their jobs simply for the paycheck will soon find themselves burned out and disillusioned. In today's world, people are taking jobs that serve as an extension of their personal convictions; they are doing the things that give their

> ONLY THE THINGS THAT ACCOMPLISH OUR EXPRESSED PURPOSE (OR PURPOSES) GET THE PRIVILEGE OF OUR ATTENTION, EVERYTHING ELSE IS JETTISONED.

lives purpose. People want meaningful lives (a nice paycheck can be an added benefit). A doctor practices medicine because he wants to help people; a lawyer practices law because she wants to preserve the legal rights of others; a teacher teaches to change lives. This being said, it is absolutely vital to not only identify the chief purpose of your team, but to point out the individual contributions that each team member has made in accomplishing that purpose.

Make it a priority to clearly define the roles of your team members as they pertain to the working environment. If someone is in charge of the office staff, everyone should know that. If another person is in charge of a particular account, let it be known across the board. If someone takes the lead when you are out of town, you need to make it clear to everyone on the team. People need to know where they fit into the organizational puzzle in order to feel that they are contributing members of your team.

I think one of the most difficult positions for someone to fill on a professional football team is the role of the place kicker. That's right—the kicker! I wouldn't say it is the toughest position, but surely one of the most difficult. Think about it. When you are a running back, a quarterback, a wide receiver, a safety, a corner, or another high-profile-position player, you've got all the attention of the world! Those players tend to be flashy and smooth; they want everyone to know their names, and most people do. Now think about the kicker of any given football team. He is usually smaller than the other guys—sometimes *much* smaller. He takes a fair amount of jesting throughout the week because he seems to lack the main ingredient(s) of a football player (bulk and/or speed) and he gets next to no respect as a contributing member of his team. I had a conversation with an ex-professional place kicker years ago. He told me that kickers from various teams in the league band together and have a fraternity of sorts. What they don't find on their teams (i.e., respect as a fully contributing team member) they find with each other.

It might surprise you that the leading scorer in the history of the National Football League (NFL[1]) happens to be a kicker, Morten Andersen. He is an active player in the NFL as of the writing of this book and continues to rack up points in his record-leading effort, having surpassed the previous record of 2,434 points, which was held by another great kicker, Gary Anderson. In fact, the top twenty scorers in NFL history are all kickers.[2] Nonetheless, no one seems to care about the kicker—until, that is, there is one second left on the clock and the game is going to be decided by a field goal. Then everyone loves the kicker! They start patting his shoulders and pumping him up with a fresh stream of encouragement that they instinctively begin to inject into his system. Most of the time, they have to take a moment to remember what his name is; but when the game is at stake and the kicker will be the deciding factor, nobody is more important. If he makes it, he'll be good for another week. If he misses, it is back to the bottom of the pecking order—and in some cases, it could mean his career is over!

> **THE PEOPLE ON YOUR TEAM NEED TO KNOW THAT THEIR EFFORTS ARE IMPORTANT TO THE OVERALL SUCCESS OF THE TEAM.**

What quarterback has ever felt that if he throws an interception during a potential game-winning drive, he will be cut? What receiver has ever felt that pressure? What corner? What

---

1. NFL is a registered trademark of the National Football League.

2. "NFL All-Time Points Leaders," *ESPN.com,* http://sports.espn.go.com/nfl/alltime/leaders?cat=points (accessed 14 Nov 2007).

safety? That type of "we love you when you succeed and despise you when you fail" attitude will destroy the morale of any member of any team. Here is the real question. Are there people on your team who are not being accepted by the others? Are they having a difficult time identifying their contributions to the purpose of your team? They won't be with you long unless you do something immediately. The people on your team need to know that their efforts are important to the overall success of the team. They need to feel part of the big picture. They need to have purpose linked to their efforts each and every day. Your "kickers" need to know their contributions are integral to the success of the team and just as important.

Remember that the people on your team need to know what the goals of the team are. In other words, they need to know exactly what the team is trying to accomplish. You need to make that very clear to them in order for efforts to be streamlined in a way that brings success. You also need to maintain a high level of purpose in the lives of your team members individually. Each must know that his or her existence in the life of your team is vital. If personal purpose is established, each team member will work harder to accomplish individual and team goals. Clearly articulated purpose is a nonnegotiable element that will ultimately enhance or, if unclear, weaken the productivity of your team. Never underestimate the power of purpose.

6

Encouragement

Highly productive teams are highly motivated teams. A team may have many important traits including talent, work ethic, and drive but without an atmosphere of encouragement, the long-term impact of the team will be inhibited. Your team will be highly motivated to get the job done when each member feels appreciated and encouraged. Without an appropriate amount of encouragement, burnout and/or lack of security will seep in and undermine the efforts of an otherwise finely tuned team.

Once again, I would like to remind you that a group of people working toward a common goal does not necessarily make them a team. Though it is true that there needs to be purpose and direction, once that purpose is in place, great team leaders know to turn their attention from the goal to those people achieving the goal. If you will recall, we just talked about how purpose, in essence, has two parts. One part of purpose focuses on your team. Everyone must know what the team is working toward collectively. The other part of purpose is aimed at the individuals who do the work. The people on your team must know what each individual stake is in the game. That same ideology is true of affirmation. Common and compelling purpose helps to turn a *group* of people into a *team* of people; encouragement is the tune-up process that keeps the team moving at ramming speed.

THE GAS STATION EXPERIENCE

I love cars. I am always amazed at the technology that continues to evolve and improve in the automotive industry year after year. In fact, few modern advances can match the incredible cultural transformation that the introduction of the automobile has made in our world. Just think of the hundreds of thousands of jobs that exist because at one point, some guy got tired of walking from one place to another. It is an invention that, though often taken for granted, remains nothing short of amazing! Is there anything better than a brand new car? It looks great. It smells great. It drives smoothly and, my personal favorite, it has been equipped with the most up to date and modern features. When the time comes for our family to purchase a new car, I probably get a little extreme in the "research" department. My wife wants nothing to do with the process, but for me, it is all good! I get on the Internet and find out what has been said about a particular make or model. I can spend hours on Saturdays at car lots looking at a variety of possibilities. I've got a lot of patience when it comes to buying a car because once I decide to buy it, there is no turning back. When I finally purchase a car, however, I don't only purchase the right to drive that car, I simultaneously take on the sole responsibility of keeping that car running. I have to have the oil changed; I have to take it in for periodic tune-ups; I have to have it washed so it continues to look sharp; and I have to keep the tires aligned (for those moments when my wonderful wife misjudges corners). Most importantly, however, I have to take it by the gas station in order to keep fuel running through the car. I must keep things working right or things will stop working altogether!

I can see quite a few interesting parallels between researching, purchasing, and maintaining a car and leading a team. Many employers do a fair amount of research when hiring the right people; it's the only way to assure the best chance at finding top quality employees. We look at resumes, consider profiles, call references, and do the proper amount of due diligence so that no surprises present themselves after we make a hire. Great team leaders keep in mind, however, that having stellar employees not only demands hard work on the front end, but ongoing encouragement to keep people working at peak potential. When you hire someone to join your team, you simultaneously acquire the responsibility to build into the

> THE BEST TEAMS ARE THE ONES THAT HAVE CULTIVATED A CULTURE OF ENCOURAGEMENT, WHERE "TANKS" ARE FILLED UP EVERYDAY, AND PEOPLE ARE VITALIZED TO DO THE WORK THAT IS SET IN FRONT OF THEM.

life of that team member. Like automobiles, human beings need gas station experiences. We need to be filled up in order to keep moving down Productivity Lane. The best teams are the ones that have cultivated a culture of encouragement, where "tanks" are filled up everyday, and people are vitalized to do the work that is set in front of them.

A COUNTER-CULTURAL ADJUSTMENT

The critical responsibility to encourage team members falls squarely on the shoulders of the team leader. You are responsible for keeping your team adequately fired up as they work together to accomplish the purposes of your organization. Your team needs to be encouraged both corporately for their teamwork and individually for their ongoing contributions to the team effort. You need to realize, however, that encouragement is not innately hardwired into the human will. In fact, often we are more prone to criticize than affirm, as criticism often seems to take less effort to formulate.

Think of all the catch phrases that exist along the lines of "look out for you because no one else will." Our culture inundates us with messages from the media, the printed word, and music (to name a few) to put yourself first, look out for number one, and do to them before they do to you. The me-first-then-you mentality runs rampant in every area of our lives—from road rage to the workplace! For as long as I can remember, that has been the standard sold to me by our culture as to how I should be looking at life. It is an awful way to look at life! And it will destroy your team if you reinforce that way of thinking, through lack of encouraging words and/or actions, with the people who work for you. You need to be setting the bar high in the area of encouragement as it relates to your team.

> IT TAKES SO LITTLE TO TURN SOMEONE'S DAY AROUND.

It takes so little to turn someone's day around. I lean into offices all the time and say things like "Erin, great job this past week. I really think you got your point across at that meeting, and it was obvious that the people there got excited to follow you down that road. Thanks for all your hard work." I could let Erin believe that in doing good work, she is merely filling the minimum requirements of working on my team. I could grudgingly acknowledge in as few words as possible when annual review time comes around, that she does "pretty good work." I could take that approach to my team but it would be utterly foolish. Erin is a hard worker and I know that she respects my leadership, so hearing a few words of encouragement will go a long way in keeping her motivated to the great work she is capable of. I'm careful not to be gratuitous in my encouragement, but I try very hard to never let a good opportunity for encouragement slip through my fingers. Simple words of encouragement keep people motivated and running strong. Affirmation is the best tool I have found for encouraging a person on my team who has experienced a failure as the result of an idea gone sour and for keeping people from jumping ship during stressful, high-pressure times that are sure to come in any organization.

> WHEN I SET A GOOD MODEL OF ENCOURAGEMENT FOR THOSE PEOPLE WHO SERVE ON MY TEAM, THEY GO AND DO THE SAME FOR THEIR TEAMS, AS WELL AS FOR EACH OTHER.

CONTAGIOUS—ONE WAY OR ANOTHER

Encouragement is contagious. Your team will follow your lead as you encourage them and once they experience it they will want to share it. I have seen this happen over and over again. When I set a good model of encouragement for those people who serve on my team, they go and do the same for their teams, as well as for each other. Having team members who build into each other should be your goal as you encourage those around you.

Remember, you are the leader, the idea is to be followed and the best way is to lead by example.

There are few other things your team needs to excel in interpersonally than to become very good at encouraging each other. Sometimes encouragement comes by way of challenge, as your team members push one another towards greatness. Don't be afraid of team members who push each other into bigger and better things. There is obviously a point where pushing can get discouraging, and you need to guard against that. But in many ways, healthy challenges between teammates (e.g., "You can do better work than this—I've seen it!") may be accepted more readily than if that challenge comes from the team leader. As you instill the value of encouragement into the lives of those you lead, you begin the crucial first steps in creating a culture of encouragement that everyone must commit to. That component will most assuredly work to propel the efforts of your team exponentially to greater productivity and success.

> DON'T BE AFRAID OF TEAM MEMBERS WHO PUSH EACH OTHER INTO BIGGER AND BETTER THINGS.

The opposite is true as well. Many people work on teams where encouragement is conspicuously absent. People in these cold and harsh environments work in a dog-eat-dog world where they are constantly worried about losing their jobs because they never know if they are doing them correctly, even when the results might be screaming that they are. Have you ever been made to feel that you were lucky to be working somewhere or that the honor was all *yours* when it came to working for an organization? I've never met one person who actually enjoyed that feeling. So, why would any good leader think *that* is the way to treat his or her team? Unfortunately, it is a problem that plagues many organizations. When leaders fail to encourage their teams, people get discouraged—and productivity pays the price.

Leaders are not the only people who can damage the morale of a team. Any negative person on your team will work against success and productivity. Negative people are easy to spot. They suck the energy right out of the room with their downbeat countenance, their beaten down attitude that seems to swirl around them like a dark cloud, and their seeming endless ability to sap otherwise cheerful enthusiastic people of their winsomeness. Negativity should have no place on your team.

If you have "prickly" people on your team, do yourself a huge favor and focus attention on changing their attitudes. Don't take the easy way out by pretending that no problem exists. When you do that, your team begins to lose respect for you. Always take the high road of maintaining the culture of encouragement across the board—no exceptions. Set up a one-on-one meeting with your naysayer (remember, you may have more than one in your ranks) and begin the dialogue

> IF YOU HAVE "PRICKLY" PEOPLE ON YOUR TEAM, DO YOURSELF A HUGE FAVOR AND FOCUS ATTENTION ON CHANGING THEIR ATTITUDES.

that will help her understand what you are observing. Some negative types are so used to living in that dark place that they lose touch with their ability to see the glass half full as opposed to half empty. Explain gently, yet firmly, how negativity is affecting her personal contribution to the team, the morale of the team as a whole, and the resulting lowering of overall productivity. When I have the unfortunate duty of talking to someone about this, this person will usually ask if someone else has said something to me about it. I make it a point to take the full weight of the situation every time by simply saying "*I'm* talking to *you* about it. I see it as a problem." If this team member is one you really feel can turn it around, you may need (probably will need) more than one meeting; a negative attitude can be deeply ingrained.

I have found that people who struggle to stay positive in life need extra attention. When I'm dealing with someone who has a tendency to have a negative outlook, I remind myself that he will need an extra "high five" with an extra word of encouragement about something that has gone really well in his department. I try to persuade him to focus as much as possible on the things that are going right! And in order to focus attention in that direction, it is crucial for me to be acutely aware of what is going well as a result of his efforts, so I can praise that effectively. You will need more than a little patience and perseverance to turn pessimism into, if not optimism, then at least a positive approach to the workplace and, hopefully, life in general. However, if a negative person falls into "the right people" category, isn't he worth your effort? Everyone on your team must understand the power and necessity of encouragement, especially the team leader. Your team members can only go so far on a single tank of gas. You might have a few who have a bit higher MPG (miles per gallon), but eventually even the most resilient run out of gas. Don't let it happen on your team.

LITTLE THINGS MEAN A LOT

One year, when my team members were putting together their strategic goals and aspirations for the coming year, one of them wrote that she wanted to make it a priority to do a better job of encouraging a volunteer core that consisted of a few hundred people. She wanted to make sure that they knew how important they were to our work. When I sat with her to discuss her goals, I mentioned that she should go to a stationery store near our office and pick up several boxes of blank cards. I encouraged her, as I do so many, to keep those cards on her desk for easy access and then I challenged her to write three cards per week to those people she was targeting. E-mail can accomplish the same thing, and it should be seen as a highly convenient way to communicate encouragement, *but* there is nothing like getting something in the mail. When you write a quick card to someone expressing thanks for a job well done, it will not quickly be forgotten. I have a file filled with such cards, as I find it nearly impossible to throw away the kind words of another. Believe me when I say that your team will be very encouraged to know that you took a few minutes to jot down a thought or two and send a few lines of encouragement to them.

Sometimes on my way to the office, I'll stop by a coffee shop and pick up a cup of coffee for each of my departmental directors. I've gotten to know what they like; so, when I appear with a few trays of drinks, it's like Santa Clause has come to town. Most of the time, it's nice to stand in a common area of our office and drink our morning "fix" together. Somewhere in the course of that brief time together, I'll say something like, "This morning I was thinking about how lucky I am to have such a great team. Thank you all for everything you do around here. This place wouldn't be the same without you." Sometimes, I'll just bring in one cup of coffee for someone on my team who is in need of a "pick-up" (mentally and/or physically). I very simply hand the drink to him or her and say, "I appreciate all that you do around here." It is true what has been said over the years, a little encouragement goes a long way.

There are many ways to create a culture of encouragement. You don't have to spend a lot of money to do it. You don't have to sit in a think tank and determine the best way to go. Be creative if you can, but more importantly, just be yourself. Remember, highly productive teams are highly motivated teams. Your team will thrive in an encouraging atmosphere—and you are the one responsible for setting that tone with your team.

7

Celebration

T HE TENDENCY of many teams is to focus on a loss rather than a victory. A healthy team celebrates every victory. It is important to maintain balance between critical analysis and recognition of accomplishments, including accountability when things go wrong and accolade when things go right. It seems, however, that in reality good work often goes unnoticed while poor work almost never does. If you are the type of leader who calls half-hearted work unacceptable, then you are (by definition) the type of leader who recognizes good work when you see it.

CELEBRATE TO MOTIVATE

In order to assess and identify whether or not you are celebrating your dynamic and energized team, ask yourself the following questions.

1. What do you do when you see great work accomplished by individuals on your team?

2. What do you do when your team accomplishes a stated goal?

3. How do you respond when productivity is high and your team is experiencing success?

Because of their similar natures, encouragement and celebration often go hand in hand. The difference between the two is that encouragement is something that should be happening along the road to success, while celebration is what you do when you reach your destination (success). In most cases, organizations that are missing one (encouragement) are also missing the other (celebration). However, leaders who celebrate success know what a tremendous tool celebration is in motivating their teams to even greater levels of success. Make no mistake, your team needs motivation and nothing motivates a team to get to the end of the proverbial rainbow more than the thought of the pot of gold waiting for them there. Though you probably won't offer gold bullion for a job well done, I can make you this promise—if you reward hard work, you will see more of it.

> LEADERS WHO CELEBRATE SUCCESS KNOW WHAT A TREMENDOUS TOOL CELEBRATION IS IN MOTIVATING THEIR TEAMS TO EVEN GREATER LEVELS OF SUCCESS.

To that end, the business world can learn much from the world of professional sports in the area of team celebration. When a victory (especially a big one) is experienced in sports, celebrations of the best kind ensue. Think of all the midcourt dog piles, the locker room champagne showers, the hug fests on the pitcher's mound, the buckets of ice cold water being dumped over the heads of coaches—and the list goes on and on. Few celebrations can top those enjoyed by professional athletes.

The great thing about sports teams, however, is that they don't necessarily have to win "the big game" to celebrate success. Sure, the madness is even sweeter after the World Series or the Superbowl, but doesn't the celebration look just as thrilling after a team beats their cross-town rival? Don't you love to see a field goal kicked, scored, and celebrated by a team and their home crowd—in the middle of a season? When something great happens—no matter how big or small—good teams light the fire of celebration. In sports a win is a win!

> IF THE PEOPLE ON YOUR TEAM ONLY SUCCEED TO BE GIVEN ANOTHER TASK *BEFORE* THEY ARE CELEBRATED FOR THEIR DILIGENCE, THEY WILL ENTER INTO THE NEXT PROJECT WITH A BIT LESS ENERGY FOR THE TASK.

Do you celebrate your victories? I'm not advocating that your team spray champagne all over each other after a hard day's work but there needs to be a time when you, as the leader, shower your team with the type of celebration that conveys to them that you are satisfied and pleased with what has been accomplished. A great team is always working to bring success to the organization it serves. But if the people on your team only succeed to be given another task *before* they are celebrated for their diligence, they will enter into the next project with a bit less energy for the task. For this reason, great leaders are always on high alert for ways to celebrate the hard work of their teams. When great work is accomplished, don't miss the opportunity to congratulate your team by celebrating their success.

GALVANIZING A VICTORY

People love to celebrate, and when your team gets to savor the victory through celebrating their success, they will want more of both! Celebration will whet the appetites of those on your team and push them to greater levels of productivity. The converse can also be said—*not* celebrating victories is deflating. To work hard and meet expectations (or even go beyond them) and have no celebration for those achievements can be discouraging, and if allowed to continue, demoralizing. Celebration, by its nature, brings out the best in everyone and creates a team-driven environment. It actually helps develop the other core essentials (environment, camaraderie, respect, purpose, and encouragement), and effectively builds a highly productive team. When you celebrate with your team, you convey that you care about them and are keenly aware of their efforts.

I expect a lot from those on my team. If I see something that needs attention, I will call the department head into my office and explain my position. If I see work that looks like it was put together with anything less than 100 percent of a person's energy, I'll send it back for revision. I am not mean-spirited about it, but we maintain a high level of excellence in our office, and I am responsible for holding my team to that level of excellence. On the other hand, when a job is done well, I am the first (or at least try to be the first) to congratulate and give credit where credit is due. Sometimes the celebration comes in the form of a simple lunch with my team. At other times it calls for a little more creativity and festivity.

One time, after a busy season that ushered in great success, my wife and I had all of my staff and their spouses over to our home for dinner. Afterwards, we all got into cars and went to a nice movie theatre where we took in a show together. I had already purchased the tickets and waited at the register in the concession line for everyone to get whatever they needed to ensure that the movie was well enjoyed. At the end of the night, I had spent a few hundred dollars. However, after receiving several apprecia-tive e-mails from my team in the days that followed, it was clear that my small investment paid large dividends. That particular night, my goal was to celebrate a prior team success. As a result of our time together, however, I not only conveyed my sincere

> **FAILING TO CELEBRATE A VICTORY IS LIKE LEAVING THE PUNCTUATION MARK OFF OF THE END OF A SENTENCE.**

thanks to the team, but my celebration of their success served to energize them towards further accomplishment, and invigorated them to achieve both long- and short-term team goals.

I am always amazed when I speak with people involved in very productive organizations where success is rarely celebrated, if it is celebrated at all. These organizations have paid the price over the years for not building this essential into the lifeblood of their teams. Their people are burned out, not because of the hard work, but as a result of the discouragement of being highly undervalued. They work hard, but it is clear to me, within a few minutes of speaking with them, that they have no long-term plans to stay with their particular company. What a waste! It takes so little to celebrate a job well done, and unfortunately, very few leaders actually do it. Failing to celebrate a victory is like leaving the punctuation mark off of the end of a sentence. It presents a situation that is incomplete; there is a missing ele-ment and I am convinced that element is celebration.

Team leaders are responsible for keeping a team on course. They are the guardians of the goal. It falls to you, the team leader, to do whatever is necessary to ensure that the team stays focused and energized. Do not neglect your final responsibility as it pertains to any project being handled by your team. If the job is done well and meets or exceeds expectations, do whatever it takes to communicate to your team that they accomplished the goal and you are proud of them. It will be yet another opportunity for your team to grow closer to together. During the course of accomplishing a major goal, your team will have to overcome adversities of many kinds—especially personality issues between them. When you celebrate as a team, those personality conflicts fade to black. Celebration allows a team to forget the difficult problems that are behind them and move forward onto the next big thing—together.

A PERSONAL TOUCH

Celebrating the success of an individual is equally important. It is vital that individual achievements be publicly recognized for contributing to the success of the team. If one person has a larger or more significant stake in a given project that contributes to a team success, do not let it slip the attention of the rest of the team. I have found that every project will likely have a most valuable player (MVP). Talking about an MVP is more familiar in the context of a sports team, but the same is true for any team, no matter what the business. Often a team project will produce several MVPs, but each team project will have at least one. Most of the time, the MVP will be different from one project to the next. Whatever the case, when someone shines brightly in her contribution to the endeavors of the team, she needs to be recognized. It is not favoritism to point out a person who has worked especially hard to bring victory to the team. On

> IF ONE PERSON HAS A LARGER OR MORE SIGNIFICANT STAKE IN A GIVEN PROJECT THAT CONTRIBUTES TO A TEAM SUCCESS, DO NOT LET IT SLIP THE ATTENTION OF THE REST OF THE TEAM.

the contrary, it is unreasonable to let the significant work of an individual go unrecognized. If someone is helping you keep the standard of excellence very high, make it known to the entire team.

Let me discuss briefly how I approach critical analysis of individual team members versus celebrating individuals who have significantly contributed to team accomplishments. I strongly believe that problems should be dealt with privately and successes should be celebrated publicly. You may need to speak to one (or maybe a few) of your team members with regard to certain problems you have observed; others of them might be deserving of recognition for a job well done. When you need to speak to someone on your team about a negative attitude or otherwise poor quality of work being produced, do not have that conversation in a large group context. For some reason, certain leaders feel it is better to be general when confronting a problem in an organization. A memo goes out or an issue is brought up (without naming names) in a big meeting that leaves the entire group thinking, "I wonder if he was talking about me." If you need to confront a problem, do it only with the person (or people) who are directly involved. The opposite is true when celebrating the achievements of a single person on your team. When someone does great work, don't merely drop by the person's office to thank and congratulate him (though to do that is very important), make sure the entire office knows what he has done. Don't confuse the forums. Remember, problems are dealt with privately and successes are celebrated publicly.

> REMEMBER, PROBLEMS ARE DEALT WITH PRIVATELY AND SUCCESSES ARE CELEBRATED PUBLICLY.

TOASTING COHESIVENESS

Celebration is great for your team, but it is also very important for you, the team leader. Don't forget that *you* get to enjoy the celebration as well. If you take the time to celebrate victories with your team, your attitude will be better and you will enjoy your work more. Don't be afraid to let your team see you as a normal human being. Too many leaders believe that if their teams find out they are human, the team will respect them less. That is simply not true. Your team deserves to have a leader who is just as in touch with them as he expects them to be with each other.

During a celebration, all roles disappear. On a sports team, you cannot differentiate between starters and third stringers. You cannot distinguish the celebration of the coaching staff from that of the players. For a brief moment in time, every single person on the team is on the same level. When you celebrate with your team, you allow them a great opportunity to see you in a very important light. It is true, a new day will come and organizational order will be reinstated but for the moment—be it at a lunch, in a locker room, or in a ballroom—celebrate the victory together as a team.

> GREAT TEAMS CELEBRATE EVERY WIN.

Remember that great teams celebrate every win. You don't need to spend money to create a celebration. Celebration simply means taking the time necessary to recognize the victory. Don't let *one* victory slip by you or your team, enjoy every opportunity for celebration. Then once the celebration is complete, you return to your role as the leader. The efforts of your team must be refocused on the new goal and all attention must be given to that objective. Your team will feel a new sense of cohesiveness and energy as they move toward the next success and celebration.

A Final Thought

A<small>N ORGANIZED</small>, motivated, highly effective team is a thing of beauty. When a *group* of people become a *team* of people, they seem virtually unstoppable. However, the fact is that building a highly productive team takes hard work. The six essentials discussed in this book are meant to be building blocks for you, the team leader, to use in order to build new determination and efficacy into your team. You will enjoy bigger and better things as an organization if these concepts can be understood and assimilated by every person on your team. The power is in your hands, you can either remain the director of a group of people who merely work together or become the leader of an unstoppable force.

Productive teams work in great environments, they build camaraderie, they respect each other, they have purpose, personally and collectively, and they encourage one another and celebrate (and are celebrated) when any goal is reached. When morale is up so is productivity. Your team will thrive as you provide the essentials that will encourage focus and give them energy for the success that will surely come.

I am very thankful for the teams I have been a part of. Each of them has added to my perspective on leadership. There is a feeling of anticipation and enjoyment when you go to work each day loving the people you work with. There is something about working with a finely tuned team that brings an extra dose of passion and energy for the day's tasks. Do you have that passion? Do you have that energy? Everyone would agree that organizational success comes about when people work hard—and team work makes hard work easier. You will not sacrifice productivity by investing the time it takes to adopt the six essentials found in this book. In fact, the time you spend building a cohesive, synergistic team will pay your organization exponentially in dividends. Take your role as the team leader very seriously. Build your team so that each of them not only enjoys working hard every day but also enjoys the thrill of working together as an inspiring and inspired highly productive team.

Appendix A

Strategies and Goals Worksheet 2009

1. Clearly state, in fifteen (15) words or less, two to four top-tier departmental goals for 2009.

2. One by one, give a more detailed plan for accomplishing these goals.

3. For each goal listed above, state how it accomplishes the overall purpose of our organization.

4. Will there be strategic change in your department this year in any capacity? If so, explain the change and why it is going to occur.

5. Will you provide any type of departmental staff training in 2009?

6. What is a leadership principle you will personally grow in or refine throughout the year?

7. What season (summer, fall, winter, spring) will you consider to be the most important/strategic for your department? Why?

8. If you could have ANY "wish list" item that would be helpful in bringing departmental success, what would it be and how would it help?

www.ingramcontent.com/pod-product-compliance
Lightning Source LLC
Chambersburg PA
CBHW071233290326
41931CB00037B/2880